DK READERS

Level 1

A Day at Greenhill Farm
Truck Trouble
Tale of a Tadpole
Surprise Puppy!
Duckling Days
A Day at Seagull Beach
Whatever the Weather
Busy Buzzy Bee
Big Machines
Wild Baby Animals
A Bed for the Winter
Born to be a Butterfly
Dinosaur's Day
Feeding Time
Diving Dolphin
Rockets and Spaceships
My Cat's Secret
First Day at Gymnastics
A Trip to the Zoo
I Can Swim!
A Trip to the Library
A Trip to the Doctor
A Trip to the Dentist
I Want to be a Ballerina
Animal Hide and Seek
Submarines and Submersibles

Animals at Home
Let's Play Soccer
Homes Around the World
LEGO: Trouble at the Bridge
LEGO: Secret at Dolphin Bay
Star Wars: What is a Wookie?
Star Wars: Ready, Set, Podrace!
Star Wars: Luke Skywalker's Amazing Story
Star Wars Clone Wars: Watch Out for Jabba
  the Hutt!
Star Wars Clone Wars: Pirates... and Worse
Power Rangers: Jungle Fury: We are the
  Power Rangers
Lego Duplo: Around Town
Indiana Jones: Indy's Adventures
John Deere: Good Morning, Farm!
A Day in the Life of a Builder
A Day in the Life of a Dancer
A Day in the Life of a Firefighter
A Day in the Life of a Teacher
A Day in the Life of a Musician
A Day in the Life of a Doctor
A Day in the Life of a Police Officer
A Day in the Life of a TV Reporter
Gigantes de Hierro *en español*
Crías del mundo animal *en español*

Level 2

Dinosaur Dinners
Fire Fighter!
Bugs! Bugs! Bugs!
Slinky, Scaly Snakes!
Animal Hospital
The Little Ballerina
Munching, Crunching, Sniffing,
  and Snooping
The Secret Life of Trees
Winking, Blinking, Wiggling, and Waggling
Astronaut: Living in Space
Twisters!
Holiday! Celebration Days around the World
The Story of Pocahontas
Horse Show
Survivors: The Night the Titanic Sank
Eruption! The Story of Volcanoes
The Story of Columbus
Journey of a Humpback Whale
Amazing Buildings
Feathers, Flippers, and Feet
Outback Adventure: Australian Vacation
Sniffles, Sneezes, Hiccups, and Coughs
Ice Skating Stars
Let's Go Riding
I Want to Be a Gymnast

Starry Sky
Earth Smart: How to Take Care
  of the Environment
Water Everywhere
Telling Time
A Trip to the Theater
Journey of a Pioneer
Inauguration Day
Star Wars: Journey Through Space
Star Wars: A Queen's Diary
Star Wars: R2-D2 and Friends
Star Wars: Jedi in Training
Star Wars Clone Wars: Anakin in Action!
Star Wars Clone Wars: Stand Aside – Bounty
  Hunters!
Star Wars: Join the Rebels
WWE: John Cena
Spider-Man: Worst Enemies
Power Rangers: Great Adventures
Pokémon: Meet the Pokémon
Pokémon: Meet Ash!
Meet the X-Men
Indiana Jones: Traps and Snares
¡Insectos! *en español*
¡Bomberos! *en español*
La Historia de Pocahontas *en español*

A Note to Parents

DK READERS is a compelling program for beginning readers, designed in conjunction with leading literacy experts, including Dr. Linda Gambrell, Distinguished Professor of Education at Clemson University. Dr. Gambrell has served as President of the National Reading Conference, the College Reading Association, and the International Reading Association.

Beautiful illustrations and superb full-color photographs combine with engaging, easy-to-read stories to offer a fresh approach to each subject in the series. Each DK READER is guaranteed to capture a child's interest while developing his or her reading skills, general knowledge, and love of reading.

The five levels of DK READERS are aimed at different reading abilities, enabling you to choose the books that are exactly right for your child:

Pre-level 1: Learning to read
Level 1: Beginning to read
Level 2: Beginning to read alone
Level 3: Reading alone
Level 4: Proficient readers

The "normal" age at which a child begins to read can be anywhere from three to eight years old. Adult participation through the lower levels is very helpful for providing encouragement, discussing storylines, and sounding out unfamiliar words.

No matter which level you select, you can be sure that you are helping your child learn to read, then read to learn!

LONDON, NEW YORK, MUNICH,
MELBOURNE, AND DELHI

Project Editor Caryn Jenner
Art Editor Jane Horne
Series Editor Deborah Lock
US Editor Adrienne Betz
Picture Researcher Angela Anderson
Production Editor Marc Staples
Jacket Designer Natalie Godwin
Publishing Manager Bridget Giles
Art Director Martin Wilson
Space Consultant
Carole Stott

Reading Consultant
Linda Gambrell, Ph.D.

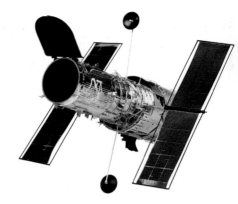

First American Edition, 2001
This edition, 2011
11 12 13 14 15 16 10 9 8 7 6 5 4 3 2 1
Published in the United States by DK Publishing
375 Hudson Street, New York, New York 10014

Published in Great Britain by Dorling Kindersley Limited.

DK books are available at special discounts when purchased in bulk
for sales promotions, premiums, fund-raising, or educational use.
For details, contact: DK Publishing Special Markets
375 Hudson Street, New York, New York 10014
SpecialSales@dk.com

A catalog record for this book is available
from the Library of Congress

ISBN: 978-0-7566-7204-1 (pb)
ISBN: 978-0-7566-7224-9 (plc)

Color reproduction by Colourscan, Singapore
Printed and bound in China by L Rex Printing Co., Ltd.

The publisher would like to thank the following for their
kind permission to reproduce their images:
Position key: c=center; b=bottom; l=left; r=right; t=top

European Space Agency: 19t, 20t, 29c; N.A.S.A.
24-25 background. **Eurospace Centre, Transinne, Belgium:** 6-7.
London Planetarium: 6. **N.A.S.A.:** 4, 5, 8, 9tr, 9b, 10-11, 12-13, 14,
15, 16-17, 18, 26tl, 28-29, 31. **Planet Earth Pictures:** 22-23, 22b.
Space and Rocket Center, Alabama: 24-25 foreground. **Science
Photo Library:** 26-27. **Paul Weston:** illustration 30cl.
Jacket images: *Front:* **Science Photo Library:** Roger Harris.
All other images © Dorling Kindersley.
For further information see: www.dkimages.com

Discover more at
www.dk.com

DK READERS

BEGINNING
1
TO READ

Rockets and Spaceships

Written by Karen Wallace

DK Publishing

5... 4... 3... 2... 1...
Blast Off!

Rumble... rumble...
ROOAAARRRR!
A rocket takes off
into the sky.
It zooms up and
away from Earth.

rocket

The rocket flies very far,
VERY FAST.

Rumble Rumble ROOAAARRR!

Rockets help us to
explore space.
Astronauts are scientists
who travel in space.

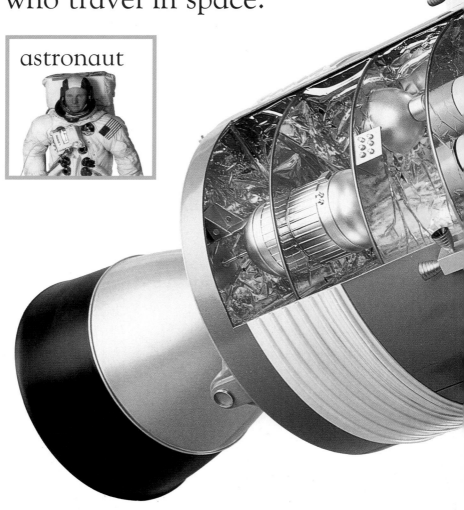

astronaut

They travel in a spaceship
at the top of a rocket.

The rocket takes
the spaceship up to space.
Then the rocket falls away.

Astronauts can see
the Moon and stars in space.
They can see planets, too.
Our planet is called Earth.
This is how astronauts see Earth
from space.

Some astronauts have traveled
to the Moon.
They explored the Moon
and did experiments.

They picked up
dust and rocks
for scientists to study
back on Earth.

Sometimes, astronauts
"walk" in space.
Walking in space is not
like walking on Earth.

Astronauts must use a special rope which keeps them
attached to their spaceship.
Otherwise, they would float away!

This is a space shuttle.
It is part rocket, part plane.
Astronauts have used it
for many trips to space.
The plane part of the space shuttle
can be used again and again.
It takes off like a rocket,
then it glides back to Earth
and lands like an airplane.

The space shuttle uses
rocket engines to blast off.
When the rocket engines fall away
the shuttle plane flies into space.

A space shuttle does
many different jobs.
It can carry satellites
as well as astronauts.

satellite

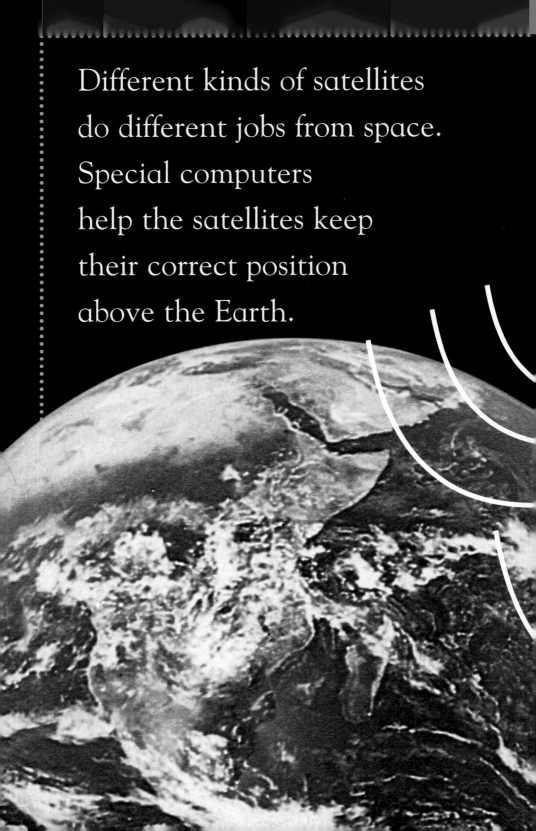

Different kinds of satellites
do different jobs from space.
Special computers
help the satellites keep
their correct position
above the Earth.

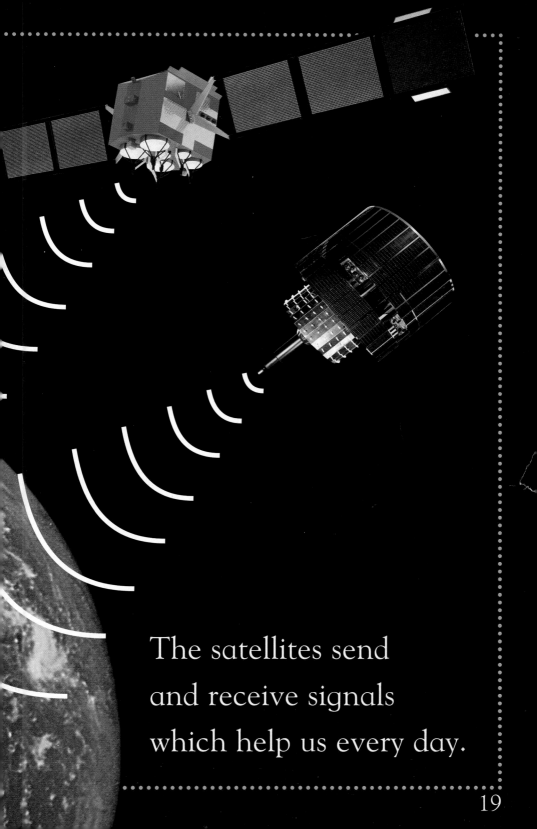

The satellites send
and receive signals
which help us every day.

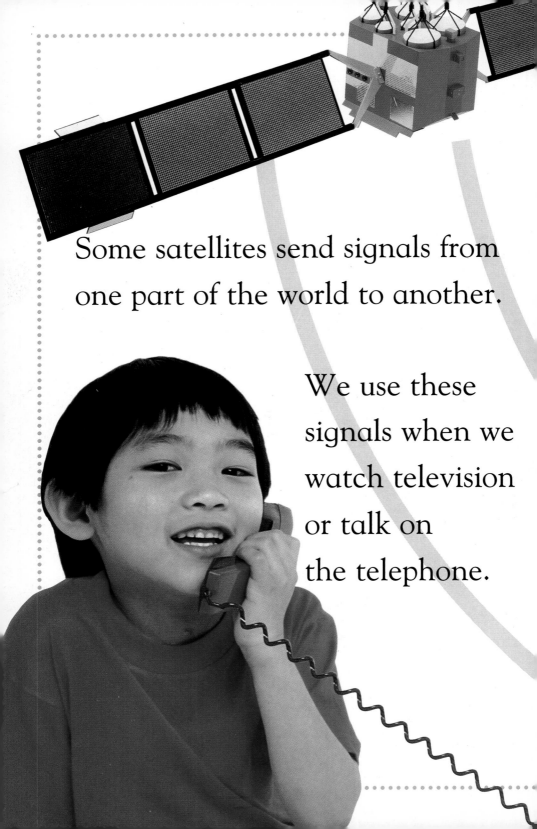

Some satellites send signals from one part of the world to another.

We use these signals when we watch television or talk on the telephone.

Other satellites
take pictures
of the weather from
high above Earth.

This picture shows
a storm coming!

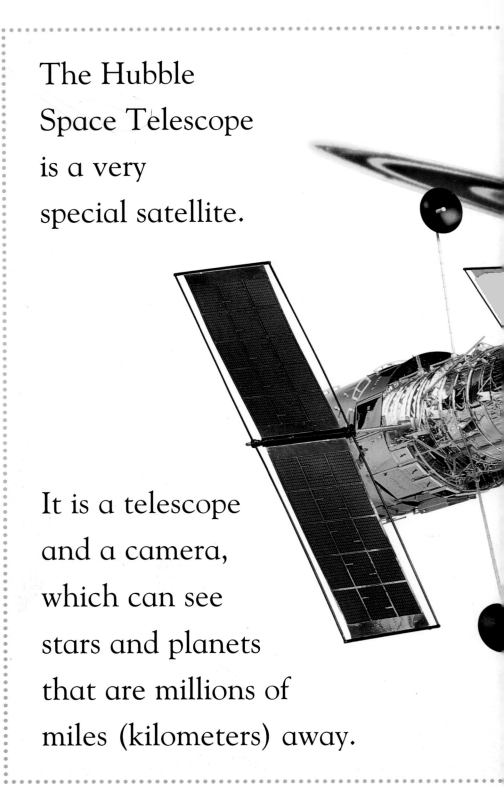

The Hubble
Space Telescope
is a very
special satellite.

It is a telescope
and a camera,
which can see
stars and planets
that are millions of
miles (kilometers) away.

The planet
in this picture
is called Saturn.

Saturn

Probes are machines
that explore space
on their own.
They do not carry
astronauts.

Space probes visit planets
that are very far away.
They take pictures
and send them back
to scientists on Earth.

Mars

A space probe carried
this tiny rover
to a planet called Mars.
The rover explored Mars
and studied the rocks.

Some people think
there might be
life on Mars.
One day, scientists
will know for sure!

Some astronauts
stay in space
for months
and months.

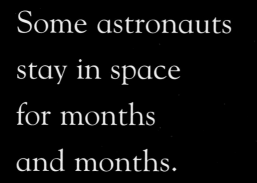

The space station
becomes their home.
They do experiments
and learn about
living in space.

Imagine eating
and sleeping
in a place
where everything floats!

There are still so many secrets
to discover.

Scientists invent new rockets
and spaceships all the time.
There are even plans
to build a space hotel.

Who knows?
One day **you** might go
on vacation in space!

Glossary

Astronaut
a person trained to travel in a spaceship and to work in space.

Mars
the fourth planet from the Sun looks a red color.

Rocket
a vehicle with a rocket engine that can travel through space.

Satellite
a man-made space object that goes around Earth, sending back information.

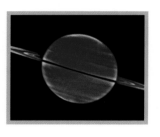

Saturn
the sixth planet from the Sun has seven thin rings of ice around it.

Index